Meet J. K. Rowling

S. Ward

The Rosen Publishing Group's
PowerKids Press™
New York

Published in 2001 by The Rosen Publishing Group, Inc.
29 East 21st Street, New York, NY 10010

First Edition

Book Design: Maria Melendez

Photo Credits: Cover, title page, (portrait of J. K. Rowling), p. 4 (portrait of J. K. Rowling) © Mitch Gerber/CORBIS; p. 6 (Church Cottage, Tutshill), p. 7 (Forest of Dean), p. 8 (University of Exeter) photo courtesy of the University of Exeter, England; p. 10 (Edinburgh Castle) © Dave G. Houser/CORBIS; p. 11 © Associated Press AP/Suzanne Mapes; p. 12 (Nicolsons Restaurant) photo courtesy of Nicolsons Restaurant, Edinburgh; p. 16 (J. K. Rowling talking to young fans), p. 19 (book-signing session by J. K. Rowling) © AP/Wide World Photos; p. 18 (Tutshill Primary School), p. 22 (Forest of Dean) © Oxford Picture Library/Chris Andrews.

Grateful acknowledgment is made for permission to reprint previously published material on pp. 5, 9, 13, 14, 15, 17, and 20: book cover and text excerpts on pp. 131 and 189 From HARRY POTTER AND THE SORCERER'S STONE by J. K. Rowling. Text copyright © 1997 by J. K. Rowling, illustration copyright © 1998 by Mary GrandPré. Published by Arthur Levine Books, an imprint of Scholastic Press. Reprinted by permission of Scholastic Inc.; book cover and text excerpts on pp. 22 and 207 From HARRY POTTER AND THE CHAMBER OF SECRETS by J. K. Rowling. Text copyright © 1999 by J. K. Rowling, illustration copyright © 1999 by Mary GrandPré. Published by Arthur Levine Books, an imprint of Scholastic Press. Reprinted by permission of Scholastic Inc.; text excerpt on p. 334 From HARRY POTTER AND THE PRISONER OF AZKABAN by J. K. Rowling. Text copyright © 1999 by J. K. Rowling, illustration copyright © 1999 by Mary GrandPré. Published by Arthur Levine Books, an imprint of Scholastic Press. Reprinted by permission of Scholastic Inc. .

Ward, S. (Stasia), 1968–
    Meet J. K. Rowling / S. Ward.—1st ed.
   p. cm. — (About the author)
    Summary: An easy-to-read biography of J. K. Rowling, the English author of the popular Harry Potter series of children's books.
    ISBN 0-8239-5711-X (alk. paper)
    1. Rowling, J. K.—Juvenile literature. 2. Authors, English—20th century—Biography—Juvenile literature. 3. Children's stories—Authorship—Juvenile literature. [1. Rowling, J. K. 2. Authors, English. 3. Women—Biography.] I. Title. II. Series.

PR6068.O93 Z9 2000
823'.914—dc21
    [B]   00-025375

Manufactured in the United States of America

Contents

Harry Potter

In 1997, a book called *Harry Potter and the Philosopher's Stone* arrived in bookstores in England. The story was about an 11-year-old orphan named Harry Potter. An orphan is a child who no longer has parents. Harry finds out that he is a **wizard**. Children and grown-ups loved reading about Harry Potter. The book became a **best-seller**.

In 1998, the book was printed in the United States. The title was changed to *Harry Potter and the Sorcerer's Stone*. It became a hit in the United States, too. The **author** of the book is J. K. Rowling. The story of how she wrote it is as amazing as that of Harry Potter himself.

J. K. Rowling wrote a book about Harry Potter, a young orphan who finds out that he has magical powers. The book became a best-seller.

"It happened again. It was as though the broom was trying to buck him off. But Nimbus Two Thousands did not suddenly decide to buck their riders off. Harry tried to turn back toward the Gryffindor goal posts . . . and then he realized that his broom was completely out of his control."

—from p. 189 of *Harry Potter and the Sorcerer's Stone* (1997)

5

Childhood

Joanne Kathleen Rowling grew up in a place called Forest of Dean, England. Her father was a factory manager. Her mother was a lab **technician**. Joanne and her sister, Di, went to Tutshill Primary School and later to Wyedean Comprehensive School. This is a state-run day school like the public schools in the United States. Joanne did well in school. Her great dream was to become a writer. She wrote her first story at the age of six. The story was called "Rabbit." Joanne loved to read. One of her favorite books as a child was *The Little White Horse* by Elizabeth Groudge. Later, she read the *Chronicles of Narnia* by C. S. Lewis.

Joanne lived in this church cottage in Tutshill Village in Forest of Dean

Forest of Dean, where Joanne grew up, was an ancient royal forest in southwestern England. An area between the Wye and Severn rivers, it is a national forest park today. ▶

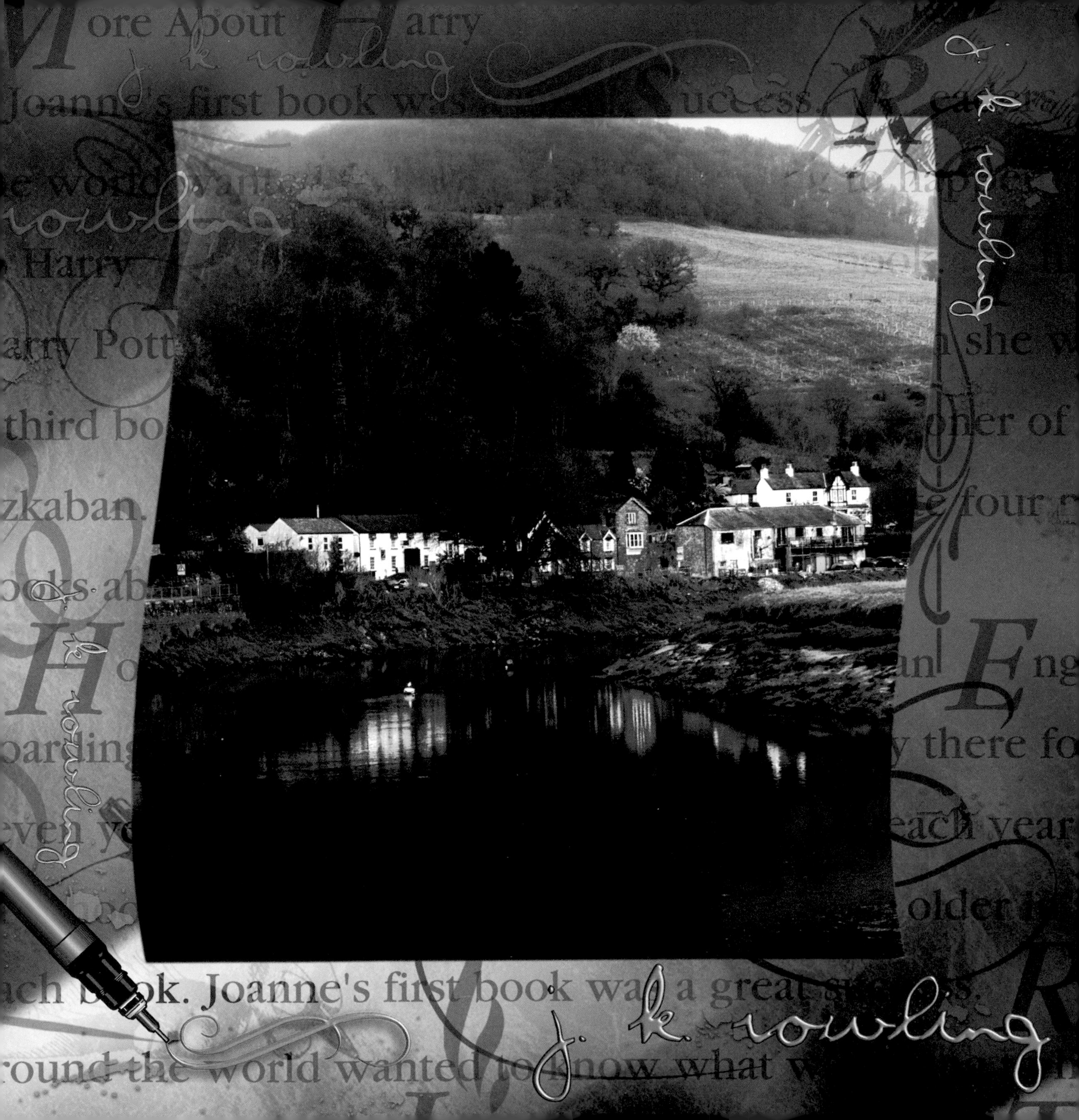

More About Harry
j. k. rowling

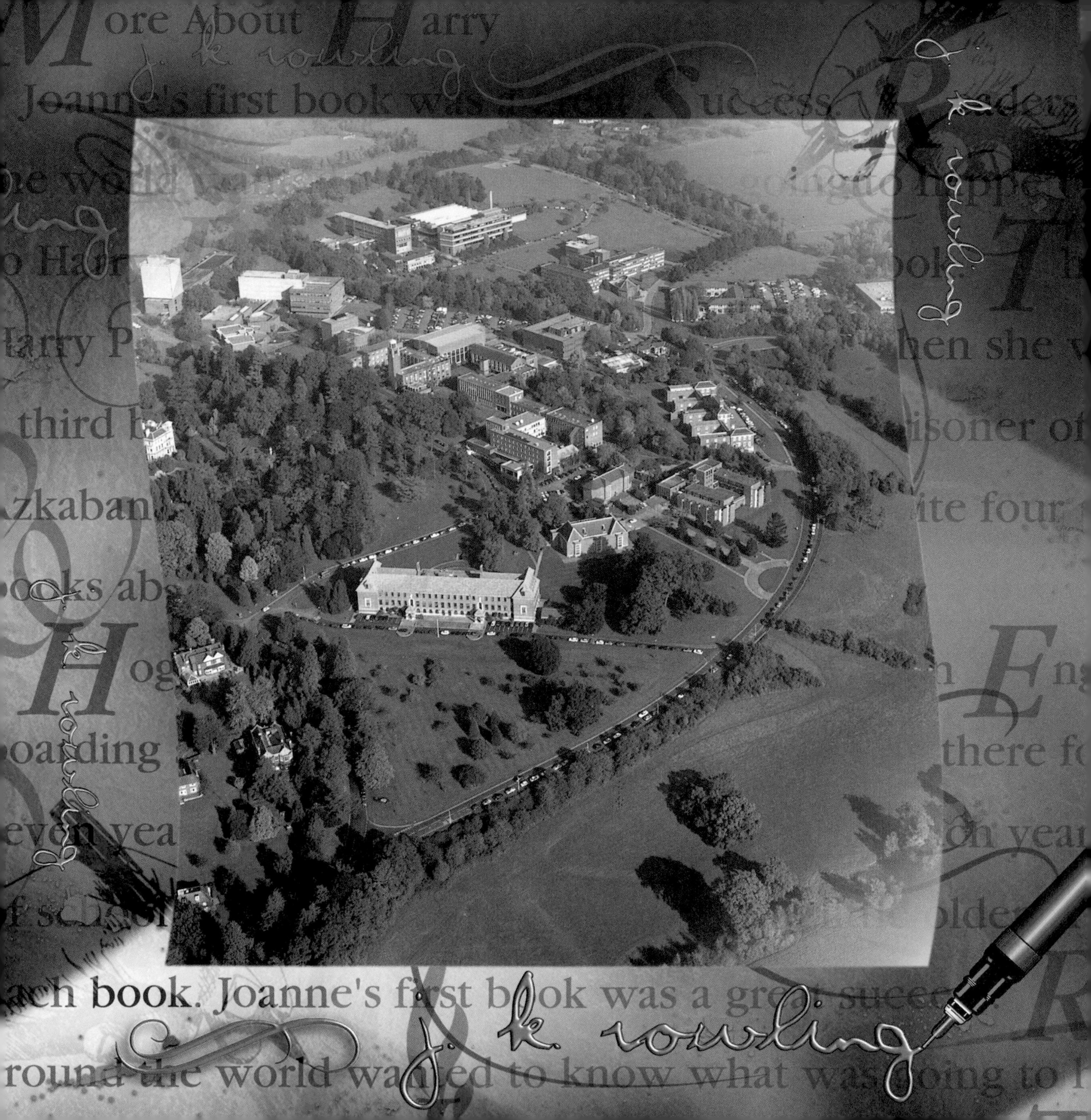

An Idea for a Story

Joanne studied French at the University of Exeter in England. Her parents hoped she could get work as a **bilingual** secretary. This was not what Joanne really wanted to do.

One day in 1990, Joanne was traveling on a train from Manchester to London in England. She was staring out the window when an idea for a story came into her mind. She imagined a boy who was trying to find his identity. In other words, he was trying to find out who he really was. This was the beginning of the **character** Harry Potter.

The University of Exeter is located in the city of Exeter, in southwestern England. Joanne studied French at the University of Exeter and planned to become a bilingual secretary.

"Harry yelled in shock and backed away into the desk. . . . . the bird, meanwhile, had become a fireball; it gave one loud shriek and next second there was nothing but a smouldering pile of ash on the floor."

—from p. 207 of *Harry Potter and the Chamber of Secrets* (1999)

Tough Times

Having an idea for a good story did not make life easy for Joanne. Her mother died soon after Joanne started to write about Harry. Then Joanne lost her job.

In September 1990, she traveled to Portugal to take a job teaching English. She met a Portuguese journalist. A journalist gathers, writes, and presents news for a newspaper or magazine. The two fell in love and got married. They had a daughter, Jessica. The marriage was not a happy one. Joanne got **divorced**. She was on her own in a **foreign** country with a baby. She decided to go to Edinburgh, Scotland, to be near her sister, Di.

This castle is in the city of Edinburgh. Joanne moved to Edinburgh to live near her sister.

Harry Potter

The early 1990s were difficult years for Joanne. With the printing of her first book just around the corner, though, she would soon become a worldwide success. ▶

j. k. rowling
ach book. Joanne's first book was a grea
around the world wanted to know what

THE CASTLE

STREET

NORTH BRIDGE

HIGH ST

SOUTH BRIDGE

COWGATE

NICOLSON ST

GRASSMARKET

WEST END

PRINCES STREET

LEITH ST

Calton Hill

MARKET STREET

CALTON RD

LOTHIAN ROAD

THE CASTLE

CASTLE HILL

HIGH ST

NORTH BRIDGE

CANONGATE

THE GRAIN STORE

GEORGE IV BRIDGE

COWGATE

SOUTH BRIDGE

The New Scottish Parliament

HOLYROOD RD

GRASSMARKET

VICTORIA ST

CHAMBERS ST

National Museum of Scotland

Festival Theatre

NICOLSON ST

N NICOLSONS

MELVILLE DRIVE

CLERK ST

PLEASANCE

The Meadows

More About Harry

Joanne's first book was a great success.

the world wanted

to Harry Potter and

Harry Potter and

third book called

zkaban

books about

Hogwa

oarding sch

even years.

f school. Ha

ch book. Joanne's first book was a great success.

round the world wanted to know what was going to

j. k. rowling

Struggling Writer

By the time Joanne moved to Edinburgh she had already written three chapters of the first Harry Potter book. Joanne did not have a job in Edinburgh. She did not have enough money to live on. Joanne got some **public assistance** but she could not get childcare for Jessica. There was no way she could work without having someplace to leave her daughter.

To make matters worse, Joanne's tiny apartment did not have heat. To keep warm, Joanne would put Jessica in a stroller and go to a **café**. Joanne wrote parts of the Harry Potter book while Jessica napped in the stroller.

Cheery Nicolsons Café in Edinburgh (see map) was a place where Joanne wrote parts of Harry Potter's story in 1994. This photo of the café shows it after it was fixed up in 1999.

"There were a hundred and forty-two staircases at Hogwarts: wide, sweeping ones; narrow, rickety ones; some that led somewhere different on a Friday; some with a vanishing step halfway up that you had to remember to jump."

—from p. 131 of Harry Potter and the Sorcerer's Stone (1997)

13

Published!

It took Joanne five years to finish writing *Harry Potter and the Sorcerer's Stone*. When it was done, she did not have enough money to make photocopies. She had to type two copies of the story. She knew she would need to send one copy out to a **publisher**. She kept the second copy. Joanne looked in a writer's **directory** and found an **agent** named Christopher Little. Christopher helped Joanne find a publisher for her story. In 1995, Bloomsbury Press bought Joanne's book. One of the best moments of Joanne's life was when she found out that her book was going to be **published**.

Mary GrandPré is the illustrator of Joanne's first book, Harry Potter and the Sorcerer's Stone. Joanne thought it was a dream come true when the book was published.

"What was the good of magicking himself out of his room if Hogwarts would expel him for doing it? Yet life at Privet Drive had reached an all-time low. Now that the Dursleys knew they weren't going to wake up as fruit bats, he had lost his only weapon."

—from p. 22 of *Harry Potter and the Chamber of Secrets* (1999)

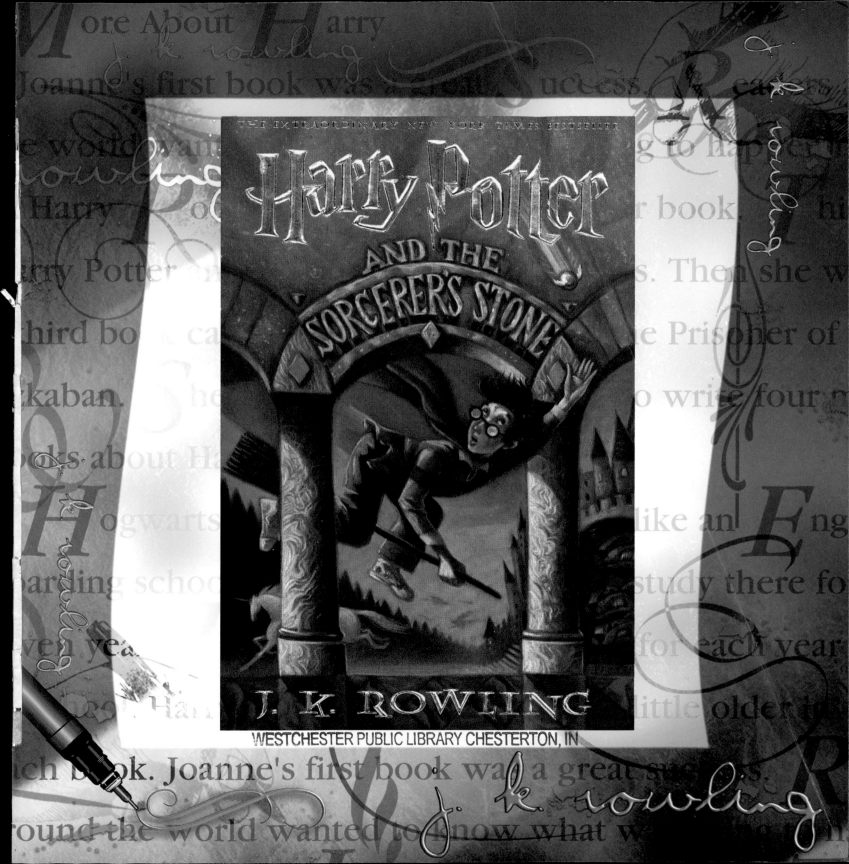

THE EXTRAORDINARY NEW YORK TIMES BESTSELLER

Harry Potter
AND THE
SORCERER'S STONE

J. K. ROWLING

More About Harry

Joanne's first book was a great success. Readers around the world wanted to know what was going to happen next to Harry Potter. Joanne wrote two more books. They are called *Harry Potter and the Chamber of Secrets* and *Harry Potter and the Prisoner of Azkaban*. She plans to write four more books about Harry.

Harry goes to school at Hogwarts. This is a magical school that is like an English **boarding school**. He will study there for seven years. Joanne will write a book for each year of school. Harry and his friends will get a little older in each book.

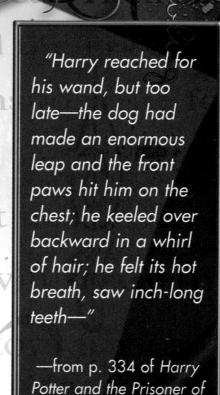

"Harry reached for his wand, but too late—the dog had made an enormous leap and the front paws hit him on the chest; he keeled over backward in a whirl of hair; he felt its hot breath, saw inch-long teeth—"

—from p. 334 of *Harry Potter and the Prisoner of Azkaban* (1999)

◀ *Joanne spoke to her young fans in October 1999 in Chicago, Illinois. Her first book won many awards, including the Best Book of 1998 from the School Library Journal.*

A World of Fans

Joanne writes her books in what is known as British English. Some of the words used in the British books might be confusing to American readers. In the United States, Joanne's books are published by Scholastic Press. Joanne's American **editor** is named Arthur Levine. Arthur helps Joanne change the British words into words that American readers will understand better.

British and American readers are not the only ones who love Harry Potter. Harry has fans around the world. The Harry Potter books have been **translated** into 28 languages, including Icelandic and Croatian.

The Tutshill Primary School, where Joanne went to school.

In October 1999, crowds of fans lined up to ask Joanne to sign copies of the Harry Potter books. "Potter Mania," or the Harry Potter craze, affected the whole world. ▶

More About Harry

Joanne's first book was a ... uccess. Readers ... going to hap ...

Harry Pott ... she ...

third bo ... er of

zkaban. ... four

ooks ab ...

oarding ... study there fo ...

en ye ... ry for each year

get a little older

ch book. Joanne's first book wa a great g ...

round the world wanted to know what w ...

j. k. rowling

ROWLING

YEAR 2

Harry Potter

AND THE CHAMBER OF SECRETS

J. K. ROWLING

ARTHUR A. LEVINE BOOKS
SCHOLASTIC PRESS

HARRY POTTER AND THE CHAMBER OF SECRETS

Characters

In the Harry Potter books, Harry has a friend named Hermione Granger. Hermione always wants to do very well in school. Joanne says she made Hermione a lot like herself at age 11, only smarter. Harry is a little like Joanne, too. Like Joanne, Harry is sad that his mom died.

There are four other important characters in the Harry Potter books. Harry's best friend is Ron Weasley. Hagrid is a giant who cares for the strange animals at Hogwarts School. Professor Dumbledore is the head of Hogwarts. Voldemort is the evil wizard who killed Harry's parents.

In Harry Potter and the Chamber of Secrets, Harry and his friends Hermione and Ron try to stay one step ahead of trouble at the magical school.

Wizard Words:
Muggle—A person who is not magical.
Parselmouth—A wizard who can talk to snakes.
Quidditch—A wizard sport that is played on broomsticks.

Wizard Places:
Diagon Alley—A street full of magical shops.
Gringotts—A wizard bank deep under the streets of London that is run by goblins.
Hogsmeade—An all-wizard village.

Keep on Writing

Today Joanne lives in Edinburgh, Scotland, with her daughter Jessica. The apartment they live in now has heat! Joanne thinks being famous feels a little strange, but she is proud of her books. She is glad that people enjoy reading them.

Joanne thinks she may feel sad when she finishes writing the Harry Potter stories. Her fans may feel sad, too. The good news is that even after Harry, Joanne will keep on writing!

The countryside of Forest of Dean.

Glossary

agent (AY-jent) A person who helps a writer, actor, or athlete with his or her career.

author (AW-thur) A person who writes books, articles, or reports.

best-seller (BEST-SEH-lur) A book that sells more copies than any other book during a certain period of time.

bilingual (by-LIN-gwel) A person who speaks two languages.

boarding school (BOR-ding SKOOL) A school where students live during the school year.

café (kah-FAY) A coffee shop or restaurant.

character (KAR-ek-tur) A person or animal that appears in a story.

directory (dih-REK-teh-ree) A book or list of names and addresses.

divorced (dih-VORST) When a married couple has legally ended their marriage.

editor (EH-dih-ter) The person in charge of correcting errors, checking facts, and deciding what will be printed in a newspaper, book, or magazine.

foreign (FOR-in) Outside one's own country.

public assistance (PUH-blik uh-SIS-tens) Money given by the government to help people who do not have enough to live on.

published (PUH-blishd) Something that is printed for people to read.

publisher (PUH-blish-uhr) A person or company whose business is printing and selling books.

technician (tek-NISH-en) A person who knows the special details and methods of a subject or job.

translated (trans-LAYT-ed) Changed from one language into another.

wizard (WIH-zerd) A person with magical powers.

Index

Web Sites

To learn more about J. K. Rowling and Harry Potter, check out these Web sites:

http://www.scholastic.com/harrypotter/index.htm
http://www.okukbooks.com/harry/rowling.htm